Just Your AVERAGE TEENAGER
Who Happens To Be BALD

By Olivia Rusk
teen author

SHARING THE MESSAGE THAT "IT'S OKAY TO BE DIFFERENT" AND PROMOTING ANTI-BULLYING

Published & distributed by:
Sandy Rusk Productions in association with Olivia's Cause

in association with:
IBJ Book Publishing
a division of IBJ Media
41 E. Washington St., Suite 200
Indianapolis, IN 46204
www.ibjbp.com

Cover photo by Erin Hession (www.erinhessionphotography.com)
Olivia's make-up by Danielle Burkhead-Wilson of Karen Hall and Co. (www.karenhallandco.com)

Other photos by Mike Taylor (www.miketaylorphotography.com),
Gambino & Laughner, Amy Pauszek and Karen Harvey Meeks

ISBN 978-934922-72-9
First Edition

Library of Congress Control Number: 2012933034

Printed in the United States of America

www.oliviascause.org or www.oliviarusk.com
Like Olivia's Cause on Facebook.
Check out Olivia's music video "I Could Be Great!" on YouTube.
Olivia's Cause is associated with The Women Like Us Foundation.
All photos used with the expressed consent of people in them to support Olivia's Cause or photos are from public domain.
A portion of the proceeds from the sale of this book will be donated Olivia's Cause.

"From the moment I laid my eyes on Olivia, I knew she was special. Her smile is electric; her magnetic energy precedes her. But then, she opened her mouth, and from that moment on I was changed. Olivia provides hope and inspiration in a world that is often

dark and uncertain for teens today. If Olivia can continue to share her wisdom, her unwavering convictions about self acceptance, and a little piece of herself to all she touches, I believe she can inspire a whole generation."

Catt Sadler, TV Host - E! News
International Spokesperson, Women Like Us Foundation

Olivia's
STORY

HEY, HOW'S IT GOING? AWESOME! WELL, YOU probably looked at the cover of this book and assumed the girl on the cover had cancer. I get that all the time and I am totally fine with that. I realize that people see a bald person and think they have cancer. Now, I don't have anything against people who assume I have cancer, in fact it doesn't faze me at all. But I am very fortunate to not have cancer. My condition is alopecia. Alo-what?! Exactly. I know what you're thinking, "OMG, what's alopecia?" "I've never even heard of that!" "Sounds like a form of cancer." Trust me, I get that all the time. Well, I am not sick or anything. My body just thinks my hair is a germ, it attacks it, and it falls out. My immune system is overactive, so in some ways I am lucky because I do not get sick very often.

I first got alopecia when I was only 18 months old, so I was just a baby. I am an only child. My mom woke up one morning and noticed that I was losing my hair. She thought, "Oh, my gosh, what is happening to my little girl? Is she dying or something?" So she rushed me to the doctor. They sat her down and said "Sandy, your daughter has alopecia. We don't know why she has it and we do not know if she

Me as a baby, when my hair loss started

will ever re-grow her hair. We don't know if she will be bald for the rest of her life; we just don't know." She was just like "What? You're a doctor, you are supposed to be able to tell me what is going to happen to my daughter." She learned that there are three types of alopecia. *Alopecia Universalis,* where you do not have hair on your whole body; *Alopecia Areata,* which is the most common and you have hair but you might have random spots of hair loss; then Alopecia *Totalis* where you will have normal body hair but no hair on your head. The unique thing about me is that I have had all three types.

So as time went by, my mom was always hoping I would re-grow my hair. When I was 18 months old I had no hair on my head, but had eyelashes and eyebrows, like I do now, so it was *Alopecia Totalis.* From age 2 to 4 I began to re-grow my hair. My mom was like, "Awesome, my daughter is re-growing her hair! Now she can go to school and kids will love her. She's going to be popular, and life will be just swell." My hair was a beautiful blonde color with dark undertones, which was the perfect mixture of my mother's blonde hair and my father's brown hair. Now, my alopecia was not completely gone.

I had hats to match every outfit

I still had spots with hair missing that would randomly change every now and then. When I started preschool I had shoulder length blonde hair and even with the spots of hair missing, just the fact that I had some hair made both my mom and me ecstatic. On the first day of school, I felt as though I was the bee's knees, the It Girl, and all because I now had hair just like all of the other pretty girls. My mother dressed me in a red and black plaid dress, white socks, black and white oxford shoes, matching back pack, and a black headband, which was necessary to hide my bald spots. My mom seemed so proud that she was able to create such a "beautiful and normal child," well, in her words.

As a child, I always thought that if I had some hair, then it wouldn't matter if I had bald spots. Well, when I had just started 3rd grade, I was 8 years old, and my hair started to fall out for a second time. I started 3rd grade and like each year, my mom met with my teacher to talk about the situation with my hair. Now for alopecia, there is no cure, but people can try and use just normal hair-growth medicines, and that's what my mother thought she could do with me. She assumed and hoped that if she spent all the money she had to help her daughter be normal, then it would be worth it. All the adults in my family and at the elementary school thought the best idea was to inform kids that I might not have hair in a week or so, even though I could not care less. My teacher mentioned the fact

With most of my hair back

My first day of school

that I had alopecia, and everyone seemed to be fine with it. But my mom, being the mother she is, was always worried. She would ask me "Are the other kids asking questions about your hair?" or "Has anyone been mean to you?" On Halloween we went trick-or-treating with my aunt, uncle, cousins, and some of their friends. A lady that happened to be with us asked my mother if I had cancer because of my hair loss. I don't think my mother had realized how much hair I had lost until someone else noticed. And that day I think that my mother knew that her perfect little baby would soon be bald again.

One day my mom came home all excited, saying "OLIVIA! Guess what? You're getting a wig!" Now, I was only 8 at the time, I had no clue why on earth my mother wanted me to get this wig. I thought she was crazy, because I could not care less whether or not I had hair. She made an appointment with a custom hair salon and we went for a consultation. When we arrived, the owner of the salon came into the room and handed us one of their wigs. The hair was so soft and silky.

My hair loss started again

We were amazed at how the wig looked so real and natural. Now, I have to admit, before we went to the consultation, I was completely adamant about not getting a wig. But once I saw and heard of all the stories of people becoming so happy once they received their wigs, it made me actually want the wig. The first thing that came into my head was, "Wouldn't the wig just fall off?" But I soon found out that the wig could actually be glued to my head, which meant that I could swim, run, sleep, shower, and basically do anything with my new hair. After what seemed like hours, we were able to choose what color and style I wanted the wig to be, which made me feel like I was in charge. I chose the color hair that was closest to my natural hair color. Choosing how long I wanted the hair to be was my absolute favorite moment. Growing up, I had always wanted the super-long, wavy, blonde hair that most popular girls had, but with my alopecia, my hair was always straight and short. Finally I would get what I wanted, and I would own a wig that was blonde, long, wavy, and all mine.

While we waited for my new hair to arrive, one of our local television stations heard my story. They decided to feature a story about

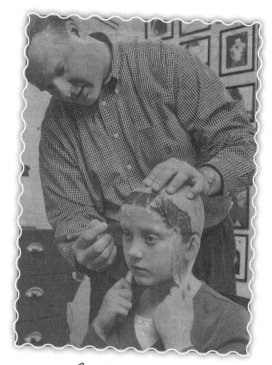

Creating my new wig

The day I got my new wig

my getting new hair for Christmas. Finally, the day arrived and we went to receive the wig. It turned out that they had to shave the remaining hair from my head, so that the hair would attach properly. I was totally fine with the fact that my head would be shaved, but it completely devastated my mother. When they put the wig on me, I literally could not believe what was in front of me. I looked completely different, which kind of saddened me inside. But if I made my mother happy, then I was happy. As all of my friends and family gathered around to boast about how gorgeous I looked, the news reporter interviewed me. Even though I wasn't that excited about the wig, the fact that I was 8 and could say "Yeah, I've been on television," made it all worth it.

After the Christmas break, I went back to school wearing my new wig. Funny thing, I do not think the other

With my mom, during the Hair Party

My new wig

kids knew that I was wearing a wig. No one said anything about the wig. Over the next couple of months, I started to have problems with the glue that was used to attach the hair system to my head. Looking back, I was only 8 years old and it

was just too hard at that age to maintain the hair. At the time, I was sort of a tomboy and I liked to run and play. As the weather got hotter outside, I found that my hair was too hot. I would get hot, sweaty, and my head would get itchy.

Almost every single day I would be late to school, because the morning would start off with my mother and me having difficulties with the wig. Most of those mornings ended with my mom and me frustrated to the point where I didn't even care what I looked like. One morning I woke up, got out of bed, and I had had enough. I walked straight up to my mom and said, "Mom, I'm going to school without my wig." My mom had a little panic attack and argued with me for about an hour, trying to make me wear my wig. I told her that I had had enough, and I went to school that day without my wig.

Yes, I took off my wig and went to school. My teacher talked to my class and everything was fine. My mom was extremely worried and called the school about 5 times every hour, just to see if I was okay. The deal that I had made with my mom that allowed me to go to

Joe Venn buzzed his hair to support me

school without my wig was that if I didn't wear my wig, I needed to wear a hat. But even to this day, I cannot stand hats. I felt as though, if I wore a hat, it would be just like wearing my wig. And I would be hiding the true me from everyone else. When my mom came to pick me up she said, "Oh my, where is your hat?" and I said "It's over there on the bench; I kind of forgot about it."

That was 6 years ago, and since then I have been naturally bald, and that one decision to not wear my wig, that one morning before school, caused my life to automatically change. People

I loved being outside, without my wig

would stop me in public just to say how beautiful I was or just how inspirational I was for being comfortable with my bald head. I started to be contacted by newspapers, radio stations, and television news shows that wanted me to share my story. I simply said, "What story?" and they were like, "You know, your story, about being bald; you are so inspiring." Well I did not feel like I was inspiring; I was just a little girl who was bald. It's not like I saved the world or anything. But I said okay and before long I had been featured on all the local television stations, several radio shows and in all of the local newspapers and several magazines. And this all had been accomplished in roughly 2 years.

When I was 10 years old, an organization was hosting an event in Bloomington, Indiana called the Healthy Choices for Girls Conference, and they contacted my mom, to see if I could be a guest speaker during the event. My first thought was, "What do they want me to talk about?" Again, I was told, "Your story, just share your story about being bald. You are such an inspiration." There would be over 200 teen girls that I would speak to, they would pay for our trip, an overnight stay in a hotel, and I

On Fox 59 News with Angela Ganote

On the cover of the NAAF magazine

My story was in Highlights magazine

would get paid $200. Well, if I was going to get paid ... okay! So, we traveled to Bloomington. During my speech, my mom was so surprised that I was not nervous and the kids really liked my story.

One day, we decide to start a line of T-shirts to create awareness for alopecia. They were called "what do YOU see? designs" with an ink blot pattern on them. They had a double meaning; What do you see when you look at the ink blot design? and, what do you see when you see someone who is unique or different? We sold the shirts from our Web site and in local stores and boutiques. With people almost

My YMCA speech

going into a frenzy wanting to know about my story the T-shirts were extremely popular. And even to this day, people will come up to me stating that they or someone they know, has one of my T-shirts.

My line of T-shirts

Now you might be thinking: What does all this have to do with bullying, right? Well, my mom and I decided to start Olivia's Cause, an organization to offer support for other people who have alopecia. With starting this organization, I was able to meet numerous people who also had alopecia. I had heard all of these traumatic stories of people being bullied and tortured just because they had alopecia. I thought, "What? Bullied because of their hair loss?" No one had ever been mean to me because I do not have hair. I could not even fathom why someone would bully someone just because they were different.

Why had people not bullied me? I would so much rather people bully me than have other people hurting and feeling worthless over something they cannot control.

I automatically wanted to help, so my mom and I decided to write and produce a music video about alopecia and teen bullying. We wrote a script and found the perfect song to use. But we had one big problem. We did not have a budget or sponsors to pay to produce it. After talking to several production companies and getting quotes as high as $35,000, we finally contacted IUPUI (Indiana University-Purdue University Indianapolis)

Filming "I Could Be Great!"

and its media center. We really got lucky, because the instructor had just assigned his students to film a music video. A group of students decided to help us as their class project. After several weeks of casting and rehearsals, we filmed the entire video over one weekend. It took from 4:00 p.m. on Friday afternoon, all day on Saturday until 11:00 p.m., and all day on Sunday until around 6:00 p.m. But we got it all done. After it was completed, the students got an A on the video and we posted "I Could Be Great!" online. Suddenly, we were contacted by people from all over the world saying what an inspiration

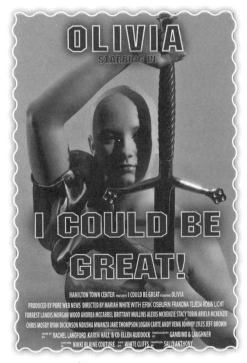

My movie poster

My Justine magazine cover

it was. To see one little video, that I could not care less about, had become this reason for me to help people.

I continued to share my story in the media, and one day we got a call from Radio Disney 98.3 FM Indianapolis. They have a radio show called "Kids' Concern Show" and asked me if I would share my story on the show. Wow, Radio Disney 98.3 FM Indianapolis ... duh, of course. When I arrived at the studio I realized that I was going to be interviewed by kids who were my own age. The interview went phenomenally. About a week later, we received a call from Radio

Radio Disney 98.3 FM Indianapolis

Disney 98.3 FM Indianapolis, and they said that I had a "good radio voice," and wondered if I wanted to work for them. They offered me a position as a Radio Disney 98.3 FM Kidcaster. I would become an employee of the Walt Disney Company, and Radio Disney, which is part of the Disney ABC Television Group. I would interview guests on the same show that I was a guest on. I was required to fill out a packet of information that was about 35 pages long, which took forever. I had to wait four weeks and then it was official: I worked for Radio Disney 98.3 FM Indianapolis! I am still a Radio

Disney 98.3 FM Kidcaster on the show. It has been an amazing opportunity and great experience.

In 2009, we traveled to Houston for me to share my story at a conference for Alopecia Awareness. My mom and I did not get a lot of sleep the night before we left, and on the plane ride there, we ended up laughing the whole flight. Other people on the plane must have thought we were nuts, but it was probably the most fun I had ever had with my mother. It was an international event and people come from all over the world to attend it. It was so funny to see so many bald people in one place. My mom could usually pick me out of a crowd because of my head. She was surprised when I was not with her because she would look up and

At the studio

think, "Oh, there is Olivia ... no wait, that is not her ... oh, there she is ... no that is not her either." I found it hilarious that she could not even pick her own daughter out of a crowd. I was scheduled to speak during the closing ceremony on the 3rd day and my audience was about 800 people. My mom seemed to freak out because I had not prepared a speech for this event. My mother frantically kept asking me, "Uh, Olivia, what do you think you're going to do when you're up in front of 800 people?!" I simply replied, "Eh, I guess I'll just wing it."

Back home, there had been so many more stories in the

My speech in Houston

WTHR News with Anne Marie Tiernon

media about kids who are being bullied and some who have even committed suicide, two boys in our area, one whom I knew. Even in my own family, I had an uncle who committed suicide. He was my world. Because my father is not in my life, my uncle was a father figure to me. His parents were divorced, too, and he spoke with me about it a lot. He was the most generous person you could ever meet, and for that, he was my role model. He committed suicide 23 days before my birthday. I feel as though most people didn't realize that I was so affected by it, just because he was not my blood-related uncle, but his suicide crushed my life. The fact that his death was so close to my birthday absolutely ruined my 12th birthday. To this day, words can not describe how much I loved him and how much he meant to me. When I share my message, I try to include how I felt about this because it brought a connection to me and kids who were planning to commit suicide. The fact that I know how much pain his suicide brought to my life, I know how negative taking your own life can be. Even though a suicide is technically self-inflicted, it absolutely and 100% affects and devastates the people around you. And the fact that one person purposely tries to ruin someone's life, to the point that the person wants to take their life, completely enrages me.

I had more offers to do speeches at local schools. I have spoken to individual classrooms and whole auditoriums. Like the kids I speak to, I attend public school. So I have seen bullying firsthand and I know that the schools try to teach kids about bullying. I don't really know why kids listen to me, but they really seem to. Maybe it is because I am their age, too, and I understand what they are going through in school. I have never been bullied and I have been asked, "If you have never been bullied, how can you talk to other kids about bullying?" I guess that is because I am so confident in myself that bullying does not affect me in any way. Maybe people have tried to bully me, but the way I respond back to them stops it. One day a boy said to me, "Well, you are bald," and I said, "Duh … don't you think I know that?" That stopped him.

Now I am not here trying to say, look at me … I work for Radio Disney 98.3 FM Indianapolis and I have been on television, in newspapers, in magazines and more. I am here to say: I am just like you. I attend public school … I have

Speaking in schools in Central Indiana

I am just your average teenager, spending time with my friends, on Halloween, going to Homecoming and performing on The Drumline

to do homework … I hang out with my friends … I have sleepovers … I have to clean my room … and I am in the high school drumline. I am here to tell you that I am just your average teenager, who happens to be bald, and you *can* be great, no matter what you are facing. Everyone has it in them to do amazing things.

In my school, they always say, "Treat people the way you want to be treated." I used to believe that was stupid, boring, false, etc., just because I heard the phrase every single day. But when I look back and think about how many people suffer and are tortured just because they're considered different by society, it makes me realize that those words of wisdom are indeed so true.

With actor Jason Priestley

With Women Like Us co-founder Linda Rendleman

At 2011 Oscar Night Event with friend Jordan and social media superhero Amy Pauszek

With Alexis at The Mercy Foundation fundraiser

With actor Ernie Hudson of Ghostbusters

With Dr. Angela Henriksen

*Mind Tripping Illusions with
Christian and Katalina*

*On the Red Carpet with actor Forrest Landis
during the filming of my music video*

With radio and television host Billy Bush

With Co-founder of The Women Like Us Foundation, Dr. Sally Brown Bassett

With Survivor winner Rupert Boneham

With actress/comedian Rosie O'Donnell

With friend Jordan and WTHR anchor Scott Swan and his family.

With friend Jordan and Indianapolis Mayor Greg Ballard and his wife, Winnie

Movie producer Leif Bristow, his wife, Agnes, and his daughter, Brittany

John Elliott of Kroger and Joy Dumandan of WISH TV, Channel 8 News

From Olivia's
MOM

THE TWO-MINUTE CONVERSATION WITH A
STRANGER THAT CHANGED EVERYTHING

AS I SAT ON THE SIDELINES AT CONSECO FIELDHOUSE, I watched my 14- year-old daughter, Olivia, get up and take the microphone. She had been asked to share her story with approximately 2,000 kids from Central Indiana during the Indiana Fever's "Choices for Champions: Put Up Your Defense Against Bullying" event. Olivia was one of the speakers, along with Tamika Catchings, two-time Olympic Gold Medalist and Indiana Fever player, who later that season became the 2011 WNBA MVP. Olivia walked with confidence and looked so cute in what she called her "power outfit." It

Olivia speaking at Conseco Fieldhouse

was a dress, little black jacket, and pink suede heels. Olivia appeared mature and older than her age. She spoke with ease and really held the attention of the audience. I was so proud of the way she inspired everyone who heard her speak. Sitting there, tearing up with pride, I reflected on everything that has happened to Olivia. Again, I marveled at the fact that all of her accomplishments might not have happened if I had not had a two-minute conversation with a stranger, when Olivia was 10 years old.

I remembered sitting in the nail salon, four years earlier. I could see Olivia with her nail technician getting her nails done, too. She loved this rare treat of mother-daughter mani-pedis. At 10, Olivia was like most girls her age: She did well in school, had lots of friends, and had recently discovered makeup. However, there was one very visible difference: Olivia was totally bald due to the medical condition, alopecia. It had been about a year since Olivia shed her custom wig and bravely marched into her 3rd-grade classroom without hair.

I remembered watching her laugh and chat, very comfortable and confident. I on the other hand, was on edge, as usual. Since Olivia would not even wear a hat on her head, we were approached often with carefully worded questions about Olivia's health. Obviously, everyone assumed she was going through cancer treatment. People were always kind and wanted to offer support. Most had gone through cancer themselves and wanted to share their stories. I was not upset by their questions, but when I saw someone watching Olivia, I was unsure if I should bring up her condition or wait for them to ask me. That day was no different. While sitting under the hand dryer, a lady sat down beside me to dry her nails. She smiled at me and glanced at Olivia. Oh, no ... here it comes, I thought. The stranger said, "Excuse me, is that your teenage daughter over there?" I wasn't really up for the conversation, but she looked kind and smiled again, so I said, "Yes, that's my daughter Olivia, though she is not a teenager yet. She is only 10 years old." The woman then surprised me with, "Can I tell you how beautiful I think she is? I have not been able to take my eyes off of her since you arrived. She carries herself so well and she has such a style about her. I just had to tell you that I think she is so beautiful." I was so touched. As any proud mom would, I said, "Thank

Olivia's 1st birthday

you, so much!" Soon after, I paid the bill and we went about our day.

It wasn't until a few days later that the impact of our conversation fully hit me. The stranger had never even mentioned Olivia's lack of hair. She had actually commented on Olivia's beauty and saw that

Olivia was uniquely pretty without hair. That amazed me. We had dealt with Olivia's alopecia for the past 8 years, but nothing like this had happened before. WOW, this changed everything. All of the

Olivia in one of her many hats

uncertainty that I had felt began to vanish. Could it be that all of my concerns about Olivia's hair loss and how people respond to her could be unfounded? Could people really see her beauty the way I saw it? Was it really possible? This was just the shift in mind-set that I needed.

You see, I am a single mom, and Olivia is my only child. I did not have her until I was almost 40 and she is my world. Though she was born five weeks early, Olivia was a healthy, normal baby. I loved being a mom and I really enjoyed dressing her up in cute little outfits. Everyone teased me about the fact that she was always so color coordinated, with lots of little accessories. Olivia had bibs, pacifiers, socks, and baby sunglasses in every color. One of my favorite memories was taking her to the mall and pushing her around in her stroller. I felt like 40 years of pent-up motherhood was pouring out on this one little baby girl, and I loved it. It was so much fun.

Everything felt perfect until Olivia was 18 months old. She was so cute with hazel eyes and a full head of baby blonde hair. On July 3, 1998, I had the day off from work so I took Olivia for her first haircut at Cookie Cutters, a really cute salon that caters to kids. There was an indoor playground and the styling chairs are kid-sized cars, planes, horses, and more. There are televisions at each station with movies and cartoons to choose from. Olivia was intrigued, but once the haircut began, she got scared and began to struggle and cry.

As a memento of the first haircut, we were given a lock of Olivia's hair, a photo, and a certificate that stated, "Olivia has bravely submitted to the scissors of our stylist and completed all of the requirements of a first haircut." It made me laugh, because it was so cute. I did not realize until later how valuable that little lock of hair would be.

Next on our schedule that day was Olivia's doctor's appointment for her routine vaccines. She cried there, too. It broke my heart to see her upset and we went home to recover from our rough day. It was Friday and by Monday Olivia had a spot of hair loss the size of a quarter on the upper right side of her head. Within days, her hair was coming out in handfuls. Obviously, I freaked out and rushed her back to her doctor. I was told that Olivia had developed alopecia, an autoimmune condition that causes hair loss. At the time, it affected over 5 million people in the United States. Though not life-threatening, people affected

Olivia getting her first hair cut

When Olivia's hair loss began

by it can randomly lose and re-grow, some or all of their hair. Her doctor could not tell me if Olivia's hair loss would continue or if she would re-grow her hair. Unfortunately, within four weeks, she was totally bald.

I was devastated and determined to find a cure or at least more answers than I had. After several doctors and numerous types of treatments, we ended up at Riley Children's Hospital with Dr. Patricia Treadwell. She was wonderful, but, even though she was the top pediatric dermatologist, she had no more answers. She did, however, prescribe a topical steroid and women's Rogaine. We began using it immediately and over the next several months Olivia's hair began to re-grow. By age four, Olivia had most of her hair back. I was thrilled and relieved! Now my daughter could start school and look like all of the other little girls. Because she was so young, I felt that she might not even remember being bald. She began school and everything was great.

My happiness lasted only 4 years. During the summer that Olivia was 8 years old, her hair loss began again. I was heartbroken! How would my little girl be able to handle this? Would she be teased and bullied? What about when she was a teenager? Would this keep her from having a normal life? How would boys react to it? I decided that I would get the best custom-created wig that was on the market for her. I found a company in our area and discovered that a

Olivia on Pie Pony and Easter

custom "hair system" would cost $3,000. I was a struggling single mom and that was totally out of my reach. I was, however, certain that it was the right thing for my daughter. I negotiated a trade out of services with the company, where I would provide marketing for them in exchange for the new hair system.

The stylist made a mold and took measurements of Olivia's head. They asked her what length and color she wanted. Olivia selected a dark blonde, close to the color of her natural hair. It took eight weeks to create and it arrived just before the holidays. Stacia Matthews of WRTV Channel 6 News featured a story about Olivia receiving new hair for Christmas. The story was heartwarming and we were very excited. I invited our family and friends to a "reveal hair party" at the salon that made the wig. At that point, Olivia still had about 50% of her hair, and I was told that

Olivia's alopecia returns

they would need to shave it off so that the hair system would attach properly. I was sick over it and could not be in the room with her when it happened. Olivia, however, was okay with it and requested that her cousin be in the room with her.

Olivia came out with a big smile and the most amazing-looking hair! It was long, dark blonde with curls on the ends. It looked totally natural. Everyone was amazed and they all clapped and cheered.

After the hair party, we went to a local production of *The Nutcracker*. Olivia was with her cousins and they sat in a different area of the auditorium. It felt so odd to look for her in the crowd and realize that I could not spot her. With her new hair, she fit in perfectly and no one could tell that she was bald. I felt wonderful about our new situation. Over the next several days, Olivia had lots of fun with her new hair.

She learned how to use a flat iron and we bought lots of cute hair accessories. When she returned to school after the Christmas break, the kids in her class did not really understand what happened to Olivia. One child actually said, "Your hair grew a lot." That was so funny.

Unfortunately, the fun did not last. Olivia's new hair required a type of glue to attach it to her head that proved to be difficult, time-consuming, and itchy to use. Getting Olivia out the door for school became a huge challenge, and most of the time we were both in tears. On one of these mornings, Olivia announced that she was going to school without hair. At that point, she had been wearing her wig for five months and the kids in her school had never seen her totally bald. I was sure this was a bad idea, but Olivia was adamant that this is what she wanted to do. Finally, I

Olivia's hair loss continued

agreed, and we got to her school early so that I could speak to her teacher, the school nurse, the school counselor and the after-school staff. They all reassured me and finally told me to go home; they would handle the situation with Olivia. So at eight years of age, Olivia bravely marched into her 3rd-grade classroom without hair! I, on the other hand, sat in my car and cried like a baby. Ironically, the teacher explained to the kids what Olivia's situation was and nothing bad happened. That day changed the entire direction of Olivia's life. Though, I supported Olivia's decision, it took about a year and that meeting with the stranger in the nail salon, before I accepted it. That two-minute conversation helped me to catch up with what Olivia knew all along. Now we were on the same page and everything changed.

Soon after, Olivia and I founded Olivia's Cause to create awareness for alopecia and offer support to others who were affected by it. We wanted to help people who were going through what we went through. We started a support group and communicated with people from around the world about alopecia. We heard so many stories of people who were bullied, teased, and even abused due to their hair

Olivia shed her wig and went to school

loss. It affected us both deeply.

In 2008, we produced a music video about alopecia and bullying. Olivia starred in the video and played the part of a teenage girl who was bald and being bullied. Her character goes on to become

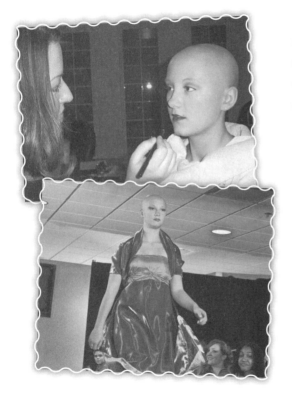

GAMBINO
& LAUGHNER

a famous model and actress. The message was: You can be great, whatever your challenges are. We posted "I Could Be Great!" on You Tube and several other networking sites. We began receiving emails and comments from all over the world about its positive message. People wrote that they were amazed and inspired by Olivia's strength. Could this really happen? Rather than seeing Olivia's condition as something negative, she was being praised for her brave stance.

In May of 2008, Olivia was asked to share her story on Radio Disney 98.3 FM Indianapolis on the "Kids' Concern Show." At that point, her story had been featured in the media numerous times, and she was very comfortable doing interviews. Olivia was a guest on the show and did a great job. This resulted in a job offer as a Radio Disney 98.3

Olivia on stage at Comedy Sportz

On WTHR News, sharing Olivia's story

Olivia and dog Annabelle on Indy Style

FM Kidcaster on the show, and she began her professional career as an employee of the Walt Disney Company and Radio Disney, which is part of the Disney ABC Television Group. She continues to work for Radio Disney 98.3 FM Indianapolis. What a rewarding experience it has been for Olivia.

The following year, Olivia launched a lecture program where she began speaking to kids and teens in schools, churches, and other organizations. She shares her story of living with alopecia and her messages include: "It's okay to be different," and she encompasses anti-bullying, teen suicide prevention, self-esteem and, of course, "you can be great with or without hair." Olivia has spoken to literally thousands of kids and teens throughout Central Indiana. She has been praised by school administrators, principals, and teachers and is directly credited with influencing one boy in Franklin, Indiana, who planned to beat up another boy after school that day. During one of her appearances in Indianapolis, a young girl in the audience admitted that she had been considering suicide and changed her mind after hearing Olivia speak. In addition, Olivia began receiving awards for her

Olivia speaking

efforts. Olivia won the 2009 Power of Children Award from the Indianapolis Children's Museum where her story is on permanent display; the 2010 Driven Like Danica Contest from racecar driver Danica Patrick; and the 2011 Well *Dunn* Award from Indiana Fever Head Coach Lin Dunn.

Ironically, something that I thought would devastate our lives has brought some amazing opportunities to Olivia. I no longer worry about how Olivia will be treated by other kids or whether she will attend the prom or have boys like her. Everyone loves her. And she has *never* been bullied.

People ask us, "If Olivia has never been bullied, how can she talk to other kids about it?" Her answer is, "Maybe kids have tried to bully me, but I am confident and because I handle it a certain way, bullying does not work on me."

My thoughts came back to the present as I watched Olivia finish her speech. As usual, she asked if there were any questions. What happened next did not surprise me. Hundreds of kids began raising their hands to ask her questions. She handled their questions openly, honestly, humbly, and with a sense of humor. Once again, she has inspired thousands of kids with her

Display—The Children's Museum of Indpls.

Olivia won the Driven Like Danica Contest

Olivia receives the Well Dunn Award

Olivia at The Power Of Children Exhibit

brave stance and ability to share her story. As the audience begins to clap, I suddenly think of how far we have come since that day in the nail salon four years earlier. I do not know the name of that stranger, and would not recognize her if we met again, but I will never forget the two-minute message that she gave me and how it changed everything. For that I am forever grateful.

Olivia signing autographs

What is BULLYING?

THIS INFORMATION IS FROM *www.stopbullying.gov.* It is an official U.S. Government Web site managed by the Department of Health & Human Services in partnership with the Department of Education and Department of Justice.

Bullying is a widespread and serious problem that can happen anywhere. It is not a phase children have to go through, it is not "just messing around," and it is not something to grow out of. Bullying can cause serious and lasting harm.

Although definitions of bullying vary, most agree that bullying involves:

Imbalance of Power: People who bully use their power to control or harm and the people being bullied may have a hard time defending themselves.

Intent to Cause Harm: Actions done by accident are not bullying; the person bullying has a goal to cause harm.

Repetition: Bullying that happens to the same person over and over by the same person or group.

▶ TYPES OF BULLYING

Bullying can take many forms. Examples include:

Verbal: name-calling, teasing

Social: spreading rumors, leaving people out on purpose, breaking up friendships

Physical: hitting, punching, shoving

Cyber bullying: using the Internet, mobile phones, or other digital technologies to harm others

An act of bullying may fit into more than one of these groups.

There are many warning signs that could indicate that someone is involved in bullying, either by bullying others or by being bullied. However, these warning signs may indicate other issues or problems, as well. If you are a parent or educator, learn more about talking to someone about bullying.

- Has friends who bully others
- Needs to win or be best at everything

▶ YOUR FEELINGS ARE IMPORTANT

Do not blame yourself. It is easy to question whether you are the problem. But no matter what someone says or does, you should not be ashamed of who you are or what you feel.

Be proud of who you are. No matter what they say, there are wonderful things about you. Keep those in mind instead of the disrespectful messages you get from the people who are bullying you.

Do not be afraid to get help. Sometimes it helps to just talk to someone who is not personally involved. Teachers, counselors, and others are there to help. Seeing a counselor or other professional does not mean there is something wrong with you.

▶ WHAT TO DO WHEN YOU ARE BEING BULLIED

The first priority is always your safety. Here are some strategies for you to consider:

Tell them to stop.

Walk away. Do not let them get to you. If you walk away or ignore them, they will not get that satisfaction.

Protect yourself. Sometimes you cannot walk away. If you are being physically hurt, protect yourself so that you can get away.

Tell an adult you trust. Talking to someone could help you figure out the best ways to deal with the problem. In some cases, adults need to get involved for the bullying to stop.

Find a safe place. Go somewhere that you feel safe and secure like the library, a favorite teacher's classroom, or the office.

Stick together. Stay with a group of an individual that you trust.

Find opportunities to make new friends. Explore your interests and join school or community activities such as sports, drama, or art. Volunteer or participate in community service.

You may feel pressured to bully others if your friends are doing it. You may think that you will no longer be popular or that you may be bullied yourself if you do not join in.

Sometimes you may think that you are just joking around but your words and your actions may actually be hurting someone.

Did you know that teens who bully are more likely to have poor grades, drop out of school, use drugs, and commit crimes?

▶ PUT YOURSELF IN THEIR SHOES

Consider how they feel. If it seems like you are hurting them at all, **stop**.

Ask the person being bullied how they feel. Maybe they are afraid or too embarrassed to say something.

Do not let your friends bully others. If your friends are bullying others, help them see how they are hurting others.

▶ MAKE IT RIGHT

Apologize. Sometimes telling someone you are sorry can go a long way.

Focus on doing things differently from now on. Although you cannot change what has happened, you can change how you treat others in the future.

▶ GET HELP

Talk with an adult. They may have good ideas about what you can do to change how you treat others.

Ask for help. Seeing a counselor or a health professional may be helpful. Sometimes it is good to talk with someone who is not personally involved to help you find solutions.

Everyone has the right to feel safe in their school and community. If you see someone being bullied, **you have the power to stop it**. By standing up for someone who is being bullied, you are not just helping someone else; you are also helping yourself. It is important to help others when you can.

▶ WHAT TO DO WHEN SOMEONE IS BEING BULLIED

Take a stand and do not join in. Make it clear that you do not support what is going on.

Do not watch someone being bullied. If you feel safe, tell the person to stop. If you do not feel safe saying something, walk away and get others to do the same. If you walk away and do not join in, you have taken the bully's audience and power away.

Support the person being bullied. Tell them that you are there to help. Offer to either go with them to report the bullying or report it for them.

Talk to an adult you trust. Talking to someone could help you figure out the best ways to deal with the problem. Reach out to a parent, teacher, or another adult that you trust to discuss the problem, especially if you feel like the person may be at risk of serious harm to themselves or others.

▶ WORK TO PREVENT BULLYING

Bullying is less likely to occur when there are strong messages against it. Work with your school, community, or other groups to create and support these messages:

Get involved with your school and community to find ways to prevent bullying.

Create an assembly, performance, or event to spread the message.

Be a leader and teach younger kids that bullying is not okay and that they can stop bullying before it begins

▶ HOW MUCH DO YOU REALLY KNOW? TAKE THIS QUIZ ABOUT BULLYING:

True or False (check only one)

1. People who bully have power over those they bully.
 ❏ True   ❏ False

2. Spreading rumors is a form of bullying.
 ❏ True   ❏ False

3. Only boys bully.
 ❏ True   ❏ False

4. People who bully are insecure and have low self-esteem.
 ❏ True   ❏ False

5. Bullying usually occurs when there are no other students around.
 ❏ True   ❏ False

6. Bullying often resolves itself when you ignore it.
 ❏ True   ❏ False

7. All children will outgrow bullying.
 ❏ True   ❏ False

8. Reporting bullying will make the situation worse.
 ❏ True   ❏ False

9. Teachers often intervene to stop bullying.
 ❏ True   ❏ False

10. Nothing can be done at schools to reduce bullying.
 ❏ True   ❏ False

11. Parents are usually aware that their children are bullying others.
 ❏ True   ❏ False

Source: StopBullying.gov

► ANSWERS:

1. True. People who bully have power over those they bully.

People who bully others usually pick on those who have less social power (peer status), psychological power (know how to harm others), or physical power (size, strength). However, some people who bully also have been bullied by others. People who both bully and are bullied by others are at the highest risk for problems (such as depression and anxiety) and are more likely to become involved in risky or delinquent behavior.

2. TRUE. Spreading rumors is a form of bullying.

Spreading rumors, name-calling, excluding others, and embarrassing them are all forms of social bullying that can cause serious, lasting harm.

3. FALSE. Only boys bully.

People think that physical bullying by boys is the most common form of bullying. However, verbal, social, and physical bullying happens among both boys and girls, especially as they grow older.

4. FALSE. People who bully are insecure and have low self-esteem.

Many people who bully are popular and have average or better-than-average self-esteem. They often take pride in their aggressive behavior and control over the people they bully. People who bully may be part of a group that thinks bullying is okay. Some people who bully may also have poor social skills and experience anxiety or depression. For them, bullying can be a way to gain social status.

5. FALSE. Bullying usually occurs when there are no other students around.

Students see about four out of every five bullying incidents at school. In fact, when they witness bullying, they give the student who is bullying positive attention or even join in about three-quarters of the time. Although 9 out of 10 students say there is bullying in their schools, adults rarely see bullying, even if they are looking for it.

6. FALSE. Bullying often resolves itself when you ignore it.

Bullying reflects an imbalance of power that happens again and again. Ignoring the bullying teaches students who bully that they can bully others without consequences. Adults and other students need to stand up for children who are bullied and to ensure they are protected and safe.

7. FALSE. All children will outgrow bullying.

For some, bullying continues as they become older. Unless someone intervenes, the bullying will likely continue and, in some cases, grow into violence and other serious problems. Children who consistently bully others often continue their aggressive behavior through adolescence and into adulthood.

8. FALSE. Reporting bullying will make the situation worse.

Research shows that children who report bullying to an adult are less likely to experience bullying in the future. Adults should encourage children to help keep their school safe and to tell an adult when they see bullying.

9. FALSE. Teachers often intervene to stop bullying.

Adults often do not witness bullying despite their good intentions. Teachers intervene in only 14 percent of classroom bullying episodes and in 4 percent of bullying incidents that happen outside the classroom.

10. FALSE. Nothing can be done at schools to reduce bullying.

School initiatives to prevent and stop bullying have reduced bullying by 15 to 50 percent. The most successful initiatives involve the entire school community of teachers, staff, parents, students, and community members.

11. FALSE. Parents are usually aware that their children are bullying others.

Parents play a critical role in bullying prevention, but they often do not know if their children bully or are bullied by others. To help prevent bullying, parents need to talk with their children about what is happening at school and in the community.

▶ PARENTS: WARNING SIGNS OF BULLYING

Being Bullied

- Comes home with damaged or missing clothing or other belongings
- Reports losing items such as books, electronics, clothing, or jewelry
- Has unexplained injuries
- Complains frequently of headaches, stomachaches, or feeling sick
- Has trouble sleeping or has frequent bad dreams
- Has changes in eating habits
- Hurts themselves
- Are very hungry after school from not eating their lunch
- Runs away from home
- Loses interest in visiting or talking with friends
- Is afraid of going to school or other activities with peers
- Loses interest in school work or begins to do poorly in school
- Appears sad, moody, angry, anxious, or depressed when they come home
- Talks about suicide
- Feels helpless

- Often feels like they are not good enough
- Blames themselves for their problems
- Suddenly has fewer friends
- Avoids certain places
- Acts differently than usual

Bullying Others
- Becomes violent with others
- Gets into physical or verbal fights with others
- Gets sent to the principal's office or detention a lot
- Has extra money or new belongings that cannot be explained
- Is quick to blame others
- Will not accept responsibility for their actions

Olivia's
SPONSORS

I WOULD LIKE TO THANK MY SPONSORS WHO HAVE supported my message and allowed me to publish this book. With their help, we can reach more kids who need to hear that "bullying is never the answer."

The Kroger family has been serving local communities for 129 years. As a company, we take a long-term view of our community engagement investments. Among the most rewarding and motivating opportunities are those supporting future generations. Olivia Rusk represents the best of her generation. She is an inspiring young leader who is changing the lives of both young people and adults through her positive, encouraging, and empowering message. We first met Olivia as a very deserving recipient of the Children's Museum of Indianapolis' Power of Children Award in 2009, but it has been a privilege for Kroger to continue supporting Olivia as she shares her anti-bullying message and publishes her first book. We look forward to sharing her book with our associates, customers, and our own families.

John A. Elliott
Public Affairs Manager, Kroger Central Division

Here at Maurices, we believe our stores should be a vital part of the communities that their stores are in. We are proud supporters of Olivia's Cause. Being able to assist Olivia and her mother, Sandy, is truly an honor. Olivia has an important message to relay to people. I am glad to be there and lend support whenever needed. Olivia is an amazing young woman that can make a difference in people's lives.

Leeca Smith
Store Manager, Maurices

Angelamd.com is committed to helping empower people to better their lives and become the people they were meant to be rather than allow social norms debilitate them or let disease control their lives. Olivia exemplifies how possible it is to change the world by changing yourself.

Dr. Angela Henriksen
www.angelamd.com

American Foundation *for* Suicide Prevention

It is an honor to be friends with Olivia Ann Rusk. We were so proud and honored to have Olivia be an Official AFSP (American Foundation for Suicide Prevention) Ambassador for the 2011 Indianapolis Out Of Darkness Walk. She touched thousands of participants with her speech and led the walk with amazing compassion, courage, and love. Olivia's Cause and its message prove that One Voice CAN make a difference in the fight against Teen Bullying and Teen Suicide Awareness. Olivia is the true definition of a Superhero. If you look up in the sky, you may just see the Magic she spreads from school to school with her positive message: 'It's Okay To Be Different.'

Amy E. Pauszek
American Foundation for Suicide Prevention
Out Of The Darkness Chair
Indianapolis Community Civic Leader

Women Like Us™
foundation
Encourage. Empower. Engage

We are blessed to have met Olivia. Olivia's poise, passion, and commitment to motivating other teens toward self-acceptance and individualism surely leaves an impression on those who are touched by her.

Sally Brown Bassett, Ph.D.
Linda Rendleman, M.S.
Co-Founders, Women Like Us Foundation

CHILDREN'S
MUSEUM
INDIANAPOLIS®

    The Children's Museum of Indianapolis is proud to help sponsor this book by Olivia Rusk, a 2009 Power of Children Awards winner. The awards, sponsored by the museum, honor and empower youth in grades 6-11 who have made an extraordinary difference in the lives of others. Olivia is one of 33 youths who has continued to make an impact within her local and global community through her winning project's message about anti-bullying and awareness of the disease alopecia. For more information about the Power of Children Awards, please go to childrensmuseum.org/poca.

Lisa Townsend
Vice President of Marketing and External Relations,
The Children's Museum of Indianapolis

AlopeciaWorld.com

Alopecia World is a unique and positively life-changing social networking site for anyone living or coping with severe or chronic hair loss. This popular Web site was launched in March 2008 by Cheryl Carvery-Jones, who has been living with alopecia areata (patchy hair loss) since 1991, and her husband RJ Jones, both of whom are committed to helping make the world a much better place for all alopecians ... one head at a time. Alopecia World supports Olivia Rusk not only because she is an outstanding and inspiring example to young and older alopecians everywhere, but also because this amazingly gifted young lady could not have chosen a better time to take a stand against the social menace of bullying. Visit us today at www.alopeciaworld.com.

Cheryl Carvery-Jones and RJ Jones
Founders of Alopecia World

Welcome.

Special thanks to Brent Frymier

Special thanks to Advanced Register
Sales, Service and Supplies for POS Systems, since 1978
advancedreg@sbcglobal.net

What People Are SAYING

WHAT I REALLY ENJOY ABOUT SPEAKING AND sharing my story is that I hear from people who are inspired by my message. I have received emails and comments from all over the world. It always surprises me that one voice can touch so many people. I believe that if we all continue to reach out and share what we have with others, we can all make a difference. I would like to share some of my favorite comments with you.

▶ COMMENTS AND EMAILS FROM KIDS WHO HAVE HEARD OLIVIA SPEAK

Lindsey Sue wrote:

"U r so inspiring u came to my school today I wish we had more convos like tht how do u make it talkin in front of crowds I wuld be terrified!"

Kaitlynn wrote:

"Omgg olivaaa when i saw yu at conceo field housee todayy andd u were amazingg(: well i just wantedd to sayy thatt urr really pretty and i lovedd yurr storyyy and im 14 just like u r (:"

Breana wrote:

"you came to my school today (: ur really amazin and ur really pretty... i never imagined a bald girl that pretty but you are(: thanks fur comin(:

Emily wrote:

"yu came to my school today:) i think yu r really amazing and really pretty:) everyone else like yu should act just the same and go along saying "yeah im bald as yu can tell" and never let people bring yu down:) thankss fur comin:)"

Ciara wrote:

I saw you in a video at my school! It's really cool, what you're doing! I hope you have a great day!

Morgan wrote:

You went to my school and you are really brave and smart and pretty I went to the children museum to see u it was really neat thank u so much for coming to talk to us

Aldo wrote:

I read you on the indystar! you are one of the most bravest person i know, i love you so much, and i want to be as cool like you,

Bennie wrote:

You came to my school and talked to us about how its okay to be different and for the explanations i thank you keep doing what youre doing their are kids out there that need your inspiration.

Shelby wrote:

Truth is, i admire you.. u came to my middle school last year and i just totally loved it :D

Travis wrote:

Truth is, you were a guest speaker at my school, loll and youre really pretty and i wish we knew each other better! :)

Shelby Lynn wrote:

"heyy olivia i just wanna say thanks for commin to my school you were amazing . ur really pretty and nice even tho i only talked to you once . but you could help alot of people with who are and how confident you are (: thanks tho"

Mack wrote:

"Hey Olivia I watch the music video you made almost every night. You rock and dont let anyone else tell you otherwise!"

Allison wrote:

"you r amazing i loved your speech Allison"

Ciara wrote:

"by the wat at the convo u said u didnt get why people thought u were so great, well its because u inspire kids to be themselves. everyone loved your speech including me ! your the most inspiring convo ive ever had"

Macayla wrote:

"Went To Conseco Fieldhouse Today, And We Listened To People Talk About Bullying , May I Say , I Loved Wat Olivia, Had To Say, And Her Story (: And I'm Sure ALOT Of Other People Did To (: , Thx Olivia, And I Love Your Music Video, Every One Is Unique (:"

Ashley wrote:

"Your speech was really awesome today when you was at my school:)"

Rachel wrote:

"there need to be more ppl like you in the world !!"

Shania wrote:

"i cant belive what Olivia said today at Conseco Field House today. The video that they showed really made me cry but that was very inspiring to me and I definitely know that she will always have that sort of confidence when she needs it. Thank you for the great inspiring words today Olivia!!!!"

Sabrina wrote:

"Oliviaaaaaa (: I saw youu tooday < 3 im 14 just like you, and it just broke my heart & hurt mee wheen you was explanning your story /: But we should talk tome time (:"

Kayleigh wrote:

"so when u talked to us today well it was sooo inspiring(: ur funny, awesome and amazing! i know we dont know each other but u just keep being u(: i still cant believe you're 14!!! lol and you're so beautiful.....just sayin"

▶ COMMENTS FROM AROUND THE WORLD ON MAILONLINE.COM

She's lucky she has a small head and a very pretty face. She doesn't need hair.

– Julie, Essex

Who needs hair when your as pretty as she is? You're doing OK kiddo.

– Emma, uk

My son has alopecia, and lost all his hair. There's no doubt it was a blow to his self esteem.

– Edward, Scottsdale, USA

Emma D - I disagree. She is most certainly brave. She refuses to wear a wig in an environment that (especially nowadays) is merciless and obsessed with "perfection." She is raising awareness of a condition that many people are unaware of. Stories like this should definitely be told more to raise awareness of a condition that no one currently knows the cure for. That is, in my view, extremely brave.

– Jennifer, Northern Ireland

What a great girl! I'm slightly older (ahem) and, whilst I have no problems with being bald, I actually prefer the term "eggshell blond".

– Toulouse Laplotte, Third Rock from the Sun

I"m a thirty-nine-year-old lady who happens to be bald too! It can be a great talking point and yes people are not always very nice and I have had abuse but its their problem as I no longer mind being bald. Besides it saves on the hairdressers and shampoo (a small but significant point!)

– Lettie, Hassocks

i can relate with olivia so much as i suffered with alopecia back in 2007 when i was in year 9 and it was the hardest time for me. As a teenager you have a lot of insecurities and having being bullied in year 7 this did nothing for my confidence. but i had a group of friends who made me realise that its ok to be different and managed to enjoy my time at high school as a normal teenager. i am now 18 and im in remission; i decided not to wear a wig to my school prom.

– Ruby , Bham UK

Great idea, Olivia. Well done. To all you urging Olivia to ignore her bullies - READ THE ARTICLE. She explicitly said she herself has not been bullied. This is very likely to do with the confidence she exudes, which will be part strong character and part excellent parenting. Don't assume victimhood. By assuming she is bullied you are almost vindicating the bullies by casting her as a victim.

– Gemma, Leighton Buzzard, UK

I suffered from alopecia as a toddler, I don't remember suffering from it though. Very brave girl!

– Kirsty, Birmingham

a good looking girl with personality to match will only be without a boyfriend if she chooses to be

– doomsayer, derby england

Don't worry Olivia you are very pretty :) and my mum suffered alopecia twice when she was your age and she has now got shoulder length blonde hair . Good luck x

– Rafa's babe, Scotland

All I have to say is GOOD FOR YOU! You've become an inspiration to others and long may you continue to do so! Well done Olivia x

– busy as ever, worcestershire

Olivia Rusk, you are a very attractive young lady and don't you dare let anyone tell you any different I bet your bullies haven't written a book . your mum is proud of you that's all that matters.. Good luck for the future.....

– Martin, UK

look, let's be honest, do you think Beyonce's hair is actually real? Nope, she is practically bald but wears wigs and looks great.

– Owen, Frinton

Such an inspiration for such a young girl! Very heartwarming!!

– LauraMD, Halifax

Lovely girl, and I'm sure her book will be an inspiration to others. Maybe we all make too much fuss about our own hair, moaning about bad hair days and the like, instead of being thankful for the hair we have. I've a friend who lost her hair during cancer treatment, distressing definitely but nowhere near as important as saving her life, and thankfully it has now grown back. Good luck to Olivia ... she's got the right attitude.

– Iseult, Cambridge

Such a beautiful girl!

– slc, London

Emma D, the best person you can be is to be yourself. Don't sell yourself short. Bullies, both in school and in adult life, do what they do because they feed on your reaction. It's time to let the bullies go hungry by staying true to yourself, by keeping a smile on your face no matter what! Look at Olivia's smile... it says a lot! If you look angry or react with anger, people may avoid you, leaving you lonely. But if you smile, people may feel a sense of welcoming that can go a long way in building relationships with potential friends. It's not easy being different, but keeping yourself positive, bold, and cheerful should really help a lot! Cruelty will always be a part of humanity, but it's never the whole of humanity. Therefore ignore what is cruelty, and open yourself up to what is the good in humanity. Let the cruel see loneliness, and may your example and goodwill inspire and welcome them to also embrace the good. Bullies need help too. Let's be their guide!

– Will Davis, Sunnyvale, CA

Good for her. What a pretty girl.

– becky, london

She's BEAUTIFUL!

– Anna, Sausalito, CA

I know this happened in America but it's about time the stupid and ignorant adults (and children) of the UK learnt that no one looks the same and we are all different for very different reasons so there's no need to bully anyone .. EVER. Only very weak characters would stoop this low so why advertise that you are one?

– zz, uk

This girl is so awesome! My grandfather got alopecia at the age of 17 and lost all his hair, so I know that it's a condition that is not easy to live with. She's a brilliant brave young woman.

– Jessica, Leicester, UK

What a brave and very beautiful young girl. I lost my hair a few years ago and it was the most devastating thing. I had an illness, had treatment, hair grew back. Then suddenly two years later, my hair fell out again. The doctors decided it was the stress of what had happened. I took to wearing scarves until a young friend of my son said I looked like Hulk Hogan!!! Your hair is such a visible thing, it is hard for people who have not lost theirs to understand just how awful it is. She is so young to be so brave and sensible.

– Andi, margate

when I was a boy many years ago, my younger sister had a doll with glued on hair. Being a typical brother I would swing the doll around by it's hair, leaving it with bald patches. My Mother consequently nicknamed the doll Alopecia so until I was an adult I had the impression that Alopecia was a girl's name.

– Bill, Brighton England

I had alopecia recently as a result of stress. It started when I was 18 and over the last year it has settled down and grown back completely. The thought of going bald so young is scary as you feel like you have no control over the condition; you can't tell whether you could end up with permanent hair loss. It might seem really minor but it affects your confidence waking up to less hair than you had yesterday! It's so good that Olivia uses it as a strength and gives me more perspective that it's really not that bad if it does come back, you need to be confident in yourself with or without hair. She is a great role model for young sufferers. :)

– Lea, Norfolk

Wow! What a beautiful girl!

– krow, Newcastle upon Tyne

I suffered from alopecia when i was 19, i had bald patches over my scalp. The most noticeable was a patch right on the top of my head at the front probley the size of a tennis ball. I spent all my time wearing baseball hats! I looked like a right "chav" for two years! Worse thing was i was in management at the time. Luckily my hair grew back. This girl is really brave, well done! Don't let people get you down.

– Me, Surrey

I have alopecia areata so I only get bald patches now and again, but I can't imagine what it must be like to lose all your hair. Great to see she's not hiding away but raising awareness instead.

– Jennifer, Northern Ireland

A very brave a gorgeous girl!!

– Student Dolly, UK

▶ COMMENTS FROM AROUND THE WORLD FROM PEOPLE WHO HAVE SEEN OLIVIA'S MUSIC VIDEO, "I COULD BE GREAT!"

Kimberly from Ohio wrote:

Olivia, I sat & watched this video w/ my 4 yr old daughter, who has AA. My hope is for my daughter to be as self confident & strong as you. You are a wonderful role model and my dd now wishes she could 'model' too! J You are an amazing person doing wonderful things... keep it up! J

Sabine from Germany wrote:

This is what I'm talking about it!!! Great, great, great.

I hope for my daughers futures that she do not need a wig because of others, only she want a wig for herself, if she want one!!!

You are open the doors for our futures AA Kids and Adults.

Be strong, and thanks for how you are

Ivonna from Australia wrote:

I just watched your video and it brought me to tears for 2 reasons. First it brought back the hell i went through going through school and then the sadness went away half way through the video but the tears persisted, but not from sadness, but from being so inspired by your courage and beauty. I still haven't gone out in public without my wig since being tormented as a child for looking different, but I honestly think that I will spend the next few weeks wearing myself out of wearing the wig out in public, thanks to you.

Thank you so much Olivia!

Shailender from India wrote:

hi

i saw your video and that is really great and inspiring. in fact i listen to that every morning to keep my mind at peace.

i saw that actually are great.
keep going like that
bye

Camilla from Switzerland wrote:

The video is wonderful, I love it. And what a great way to spread the message that it's okay to be different and that one can be and do great regardless.

/Camilla

Kayden from California wrote:

hey Olivia! thanks for being my friend. i think it's pretty cool what you've done. you have no idea how many people you've inspired (including me!) yesterday i shaved my head (im putting pics on my site soon) and today i got my first wig. later i went out with it on and out of nowhere i decided to just not wear it even though i only have stubble on my head. thanks for helping me come out of my shell even though i still have to wear my wig to school!

Kayden

Annie from Sweden:

Hi Olivia!

One of the first things I want to do as a member at Alopecia World is to thank you for what you ve done for my daughter. Klara is an 8-year old Swedish girl, who lost most of her hair this summer. You re her biggest idol!

August was spent happpily playing during the day, but crying and mirror-watching in the evening. We searched the web for others because she doesn't know anyone with alopecia. She hated that people used the "bald" word for her, even though she has some very important fuzz left around her scalp. At the same time she doesnt want a wig. And many films and pics we saw were about wigs and most of them about grown-ups. After watching your music video and your interviews (i translated) it was the first evening I saw a little smile and hope in her face. We both think you are SO pretty!! Both bald and pretty! This was something she desperatly needed to see!!

She said "mum, what IF I shaved off /lost this last fuzz, and people tells me, like they sometimes do, that I am bald, then I can not say that it isnt true anymore, so what do i say??". I sayed "Then you say, YESSS I am bald...!" My daughter thought for a while and said "... yes...then I am bald, so what, right!? Olivia Rusk is bald and look at her".

Suddenly the future wasnt so dark anymore, even IF she would loose those litte hairs that are left. Take care and keep up ...everything that you ve started! :-)

Get HELP

ALOPECIA WORLD IS AN ORGANIZATION THAT provides support and awareness for alopecia. Check it out at www.alopeciaworld.com.

Even though I do not wear hats or wigs, I realize that it is not the right decision for everyone. There is a wonderful organization that offers wigs to kids at no charge that are made from donated human hair. If you need a wig or would like to donate your own hair, contact Locks of Love at www.locksoflove.org.

If you or someone you know is being bullied, there is help! Contact www.stopbulling.gov or www.suicidepreventionlifeline. org. If you need to talk to someone call 1 (800) 273-8255.

Locks of Love

www.locksoflove.org

Alopecia World

www.alopeciaworld.com

Suicide Hotline

(800) 273-8255

www.suicidepreventionlifeline.org

The Women Like Us Foundation

www.womenlikeusfoundation.org

Olivia's Cause
Contact Information:

Sandy Rusk

sandyrusk@aol.com

www.oliviascause.org

View Olivia's music video
"I Could Be Great!" on YouTube.com

OLIVIA'S CAUSE

Mission Statement:

Olivia's Cause is dedicated to providing inspiration, support and awareness to teens on anti-bullying and teen suicide prevention.

Olivia's Story:

Olivia Rusk is 14 years old and totally bald due to the medical condition alopecia. When she was 8 years old, she shed her custom wig and bravely marched into her 3rd grade class without hair. Since that day, Olivia has lived her life openly bald, without hats or wigs. Losing all of her hair twice since she was 2 years old could have devastated her, but instead it has given Olivia a powerful platform. With her brave stance and ability to share her story, Olivia launched a lecture program where she has inspired thousands of teens in schools, churches and other organizations through out Central Indiana. Her message is that "It's Okay to be Different", anti-bullying and teen suicide prevention. Olivia shows her teen audiences that "You Can Be Great", whatever your challenges might be.

In 2008, when Olivia was 11 years old, she wrote and produced a music video about teen bullying. "I Could Be Great!" has been viewed worldwide and she has received hundreds of letters and comments from people who were inspired by it's positive message. Olivia shares the music video with her teen audiences, during her speeches.

Olivia's story has been featured in the media numerous times and she is a Kid Caster for Radio Disney 98.3 FM Indianapolis. In 2009 Olivia won The Power of Children Award from The Indianapolis Children's Museum (where her story is on permanent display), in 2010 she won The Driven Like Danica Contest from Danica Patrick and in 2011 she won The Well Dunn Award from Coach Dunn of The Indiana Fever.

Olivia's Cause is excited to announce that Olivia has published a new book, **Just Your Average Teenager, Who Happens To Be Bald.** Olivia shares her story of living with alopecia and her positive message against bullying. Olivia's mom also shares their story from her point of view. In addition to retails sales, the goal is to donate 20,000 books at no charge to 6th, 7th and 8th graders. When you order one book, during the month of February 2012, we will donate one book to a child/teen who needs to hear Olivia's message. Just click on Add to Cart to order:

Special Thanks

Grandma Millie and Grandpa Bob

Family and friends who have supported Olivia

Staff, students and the drumline of Fishers High School

Staff and Kidcasters of Radio Disney 98.3 FM Indianapolis

Bill McCleery of The Indianapolis Star

William Booher of The Indianapolis Star

Hoda and Kathy Lee of The Today Show

Jaclyn Levin of The Today Show

Donna Gould of Health Radio with Michael Roizen, MD

Ivan and Diana of the teen tv series elev8 in Dublin, Ireland

Anne Marie Tiernon of WTHR TV, Channel 13 News

Scott Swan of WTHR TV, Channel 13 News

Dick Wolfsie of WISH TV, Channel 8 News

Deanna Dewberry of WISH TV, Channel 8 News

Stacia Matthews of WRTV TV, Channel 6 News

Angela Ganote of Fox 59 News

DeShong Perry of A Girls Gift

Patty Spitler of Pet Pals TV

Janae Swan of The Indiana Pacers

Julie Graue of The Indiana Fever

Roberta Courtright of The Indiana Fever

Coach Lin Dunn of The Indiana Fever

Claire Wilcher of Comedy Sportz

Arthur Sanford of Indy Health Minute Magazine

Danica Patrick

Lisa Brattain of The American Foundation for Suicide Prevention

Buzz Bay of Teen Links

Patricia Treadwell of Riley Children's Hospital

The staff and teens of Campus Life

Himsel Chiropractic

Julie Marie Carrier

Mark Dyer of Advanced Register

Brent Frymier of Huntington Bank

Dr. Steven Wilk

Karen Harvey Meeks

IUPUI Media Center

And Olivia's friends....Katie, Jordan, Alexis, Ariela, Kailey, Rachel, Breanna, Hannah, JB and Annabelle